P9-DVO-940

Celebrations in My World

Ramadan

Crabtree Publishing Company
www.crabtreebooks.com

Crabtree Publishing Company
www.crabtreebooks.com

Author: Molly Aloian
Coordinating editor: Chester Fisher
Series and project editor: Susan Labella
Editor: Kelley MacAulay
Copy editor: Molly Aloian
Proofreader: Reagan Miller
Project coordinator: Robert Walker
Production coordinator: Katherine Kantor
Font management: Mike Golka
Prepress technicians: Samara Parent, Ken Wright
Project manager: Kavita Lad (Q2AMEDIA)
Art direction: Dibakar Acharjee (Q2AMEDIA)
Cover design: Ranjan Singh (Q2AMEDIA)
Design: Neha Sethi (Q2AMEDIA)
Photo research: Ekta Sharma (Q2AMEDIA)

Photographs: Cover: The Hindu; Title page: Masoodrezvi/Bigstockphoto (background), The Hindu (children); P4: The Hindu; P5: The Hindu; P6: Lisavan/ Bigstockphoto; P7: yazad/Dreamstime; P8: Khz/Shutterstock; P9: Amrul Isham Ismail/ Shutterstock; P10: Katherine Garrenson/ Istockphoto; P11: Asia Images/Jupiter Images; P13: Asia Images/Jupiter Images; P15: ArkReligion.com/Alamy; P17: The Hindu; P19: Stock Image/Jupiter Images; P21: Svetlana Privezentseva/Shutterstock; P23: Asia Images/ Jupiter Images; P24: Associated Press; P25: Associated Press; P27: Ayazad/Shutterstock; P29: Associated Press; P30: Lawrence Migdale/ Photolibrary; P31: Lawrence Migdale/Photolibrary

Library and Archives Canada Cataloguing in Publication

Aloian, Molly
     Ramadan / Molly Aloian.

(Celebrations in my world)
Includes index.
ISBN 978-0-7787-4285-2 (bound).--ISBN 978-0-7787-4303-3 (pbk.)

     1. Ramadan--Juvenile literature. 2. ¬¢Id al-Fi¥tr--Juvenile literature. 3. Fasts and feasts--Islam--Juvenile literature. I. Title. II. Series.

BP186.4.A46 2008   j297.3'62   C2008-903119-9

Library of Congress Cataloging-in-Publication Data

Aloian, Molly.
     Ramadan / Molly Aloian.
          p. cm. -- (Celebrations in my world)
     Includes index.
     ISBN-13: 978-0-7787-4303-3 (pbk. : alk. paper)
     ISBN-10: 0-7787-4303-9 (pbk. : alk. paper)
     ISBN-13: 978-0-7787-4285-2 (reinforced library binding : alk. paper)
     ISBN-10: 0-7787-4285-7 (reinforced library binding : alk. paper)
     1. Ramadan--Juvenile literature. 2. Fasts and feasts--Islam--Juvenile literature. I. Title. II. Series.

BP186.4.A56 2009
297.3'62--dc22
                                        2008021208

Crabtree Publishing Company

www.crabtreebooks.com   1-800-387-7650

Published in Canada
Crabtree Publishing
616 Welland Ave.
St. Catharines, ON
L2M 5V6

Published in the United States
Crabtree Publishing
PMB16A
350 Fifth Ave., Suite 3308
New York, NY 10118

Published in the United Kingdom
Crabtree Publishing
White Cross Mills
High Town, Lancaster
LA1 4XS

Published in Australia
Crabtree Publishing
386 Mt. Alexander Rd.
Ascot Vale (Melbourne)
VIC 3032

Contents

What Is Ramadan?

Ramadan is a month-long Muslim holiday. Around the world, Muslims celebrate their families, **communities**, and faith during Ramadan. Muslims are people who believe in the religion of **Islam**. For Muslims, Ramadan is the most important holiday of the year. It is about giving to others and sharing with others.

● A young boy waits for Ramadan.

There are more than one billion Muslims living around the world. There are more than five million Muslims in the United States.

All around the world, Muslims eagerly wait
for the month of Ramadan to begin.

A Way of Life

For Muslims, Islam is a way of life and a religion. Muslim people make sure that Islam is a part of their daily lives. Muslims pray five times each day. They also promise to think about those who are in need, to help others, and to give to others each year. Many Muslims try to make a **pilgrimage** to Mecca at least once in their lives. Mecca is the holiest site in Islam.

Muslims read and pray each day.

The pilgrimage to Mecca is called the Hajj. It is a very important custom in Islam.

Following the Words

Many years ago, during the month of Ramadan, a **prophet** named Muhammad received the words of the God of Islam. A prophet is a spiritual leader. The God of Islam is named Allah. These teachings that Prophet Muhammad received from Allah became a book called the Qur'an. The Qur'an is the Muslim holy book.

● The Qur'an contains Allah's words.

Muslims believe they should follow the rules and teachings in the Qur'an. During Ramadan, people celebrate the words of the Qur'an.

Muslims around the world have been celebrating Ramadan for over 1,400 years.

9

When Is Ramadan?

Muslims follow the lunar calendar. The lunar calendar is based on the **cycles**, or movements, of the Moon as it travels around Earth. There are twelve months in the lunar calendar. Ramadan takes place in the ninth month. The word "Ramadan" is the name for this month.

Ramadan
Begins at Sundown

7 8 9

14 15

On the lunar calendar, each month begins when a new moon appears.

DID YOU KNOW?

Ramadan is a time to strengthen relationships with family and friends and reinforce ties to the community.

The months in the lunar calendar do not occur at the same time every year. Due to this, Ramadan can occur in spring, summer, autumn, or winter.

Ramadan usually lasts for 29 or 30 days.

Fasting

During Ramadan, adults and teenagers **fast**. To fast means to not eat. People do not eat or drink anything from sunrise to sunset during Ramadan. Children do not have to fast, but many try to fast for some of the time. Muslims fast during Ramadan to **purify**, or clean, themselves. They want to clean their bodies and minds and think about their faith. The fast is called The Fast of Ramadan.

DID YOU KNOW?

People fast during Ramadan to gain **compassion** *for those who are less fortunate than themselves.*

Muslims of all ages, including some children, fast during the month of Ramadan.

13

Sahoor

During Ramadan, people wake up very early in the morning while it is still dark outside. They break their fast by eating sahoor. Sahoor is a light meal eaten before sunrise. Sahoor gives people energy for the day. The Prophet Muhammad usually had a sahoor when he fasted. During sahoor, Muslims eat different kinds of food including cereal, bread, pancakes, eggs, cheese, honey, and jam. They drink tea and juice. Muslims try not to overeat during sahoor.

DID YOU KNOW?

After sahoor, people say the first prayer of the new day. The prayer is called Fajr.

Eating sahoor helps prepare people for the day's fast.

Iftar

After sunset, Muslims eat another meal. It is called iftar. They usually enjoy this meal with family and friends. Everyone looks forward to the meal because they have not had anything to eat or drink since sunrise. They need to feed their minds and bodies so that they can continue to have strength for Ramadan. A hearty stew is a common iftar food. After eating, people relax and take time to visit family and friends.

DID YOU KNOW?

Some people eat a food called dates before iftar. They do this because the Prophet Muhammad broke his fast with dates long ago.

Some Muslims eat iftar on a blanket on the floor of a room.

Praying

Praying is an important part of Ramadan. Muslims pray and think about their beliefs during Ramadan. They think about what their prophet, Muhammad, taught them. Muhammad taught them to believe in God, to pray, and to think of others. They think of good deeds they might do for others. While they are fasting each day, Muslims think of people who are hungry. They do this so they can feel grateful for what they have.

DID YOU KNOW?

Muslims pray five times each day. Each prayer has a name. The prayers are Fajr, Zuhr, Asr, Maghrib, and Isha.

Muslims all over the world pray in the same way.

The Mosque

Muslims pray in their homes, offices, and other places, but they also pray in a place called a mosque. In a mosque, Muslims can pray together as a community. The mosque's tower is called a minaret. The round **dome** on the roof is called a Quba. It is located above the room where Muslims pray together. Muslims pray on carpets on the floor of a room. They pray softly so they do not disturb one another.

DID YOU KNOW?

Muslims also go to mosques for meetings, classes, and to enjoy meals together during celebrations. The mosque is often called the masjid.

Minaret

Quba

Before they enter a mosque, Muslims remove their shoes so that the mosque remains clean.

The Qur'an

Muslims read the Qur'an during Ramadan. The Qur'an is their holy book. It is divided into chapters. People read the Qur'an by themselves or in groups. Some people read the entire book. Others read certain parts. Some people even memorize the Qur'an. The Qur'an is a long book so it can take years for people to memorize it. Muslims read the Qur'an because it gives them **guidance**. The Qur'an directs Muslims to think about their faith and to think about showing kindness and mercy to others.

DID YOU KNOW?

Muslim children usually begin reading the Qur'an at an early age. It is important for children to know the Qur'an.

During Ramadan, this girl will try to read the Qur'an from beginning to end.

Charity

During Ramadan, Muslims give to others. They give food to people who are hungry and they give money to people who are poor or who need special help. They invite people to join them for iftar. Giving charity in this way reminds Muslims of the teachings in the Qur'an. It helps them remember why it is important to be generous to others who are in need. They try to be **tolerant** of others and their beliefs.

● This young boy is collecting money for refugees.

DID YOU KNOW?

Many Muslims are kind to strangers and give to the poor and less fortunate.

Some families donate the amount of money it would take to feed the number of people in their own family. How many people are in your family?

The Night of Power

The Night of Power takes place near the end of Ramadan, on the 27th night of the month. Muslims believe Muhammad first received the **revelation** of the Qur'an on this night. On the Night of Power, people spend extra time praying. Some people recite passages from the Qur'an. During the last ten days of Ramadan, some people stay at the mosque all night. People forgive others who have hurt them. Muslims also ask for forgiveness from others and from God.

DID YOU KNOW?

During the Night of Power, Muslims promise to do good deeds and be better people.

This boy is praying during the Night of Power.

Eid al-Fitr!

At the end of Ramadan, it is time to celebrate! It is Eid al-Fitr, which is a three-day festival. Sometimes there are carnivals and fairs. People wear new clothes or dress in their best clothes and visit with family and friends. People give and receive small gifts or money. They share food such as dates and rice. Families also eat meats such as spicy chicken, beef, or lamb for the celebration meal.

DID YOU KNOW?

In some countries, girls decorate their hands with henna in celebration of Eid al-Fitr. Henna is a reddish brown dye that stands for happiness and beauty.

People know it is the end of Ramadan when they see another crescent-shaped moon.

29

Treat Time!

Many people make special foods for family during Ramadan, especially near the end of the holiday for Eid al-Fitr. Some people make special cookies with dates in the middle. They place powdered sugar on the cookies. The cookies are shaped like rectangles or circles. The cookies taste especially sweet because everyone who eats them has gone so long without food.

● Families bake special cookies for Eid al-Fitr.

DID YOU KNOW?

Eid al-Fitr means "the Festival of Fast-Breaking" in the Arabic language.

Some people dip the cookie dough in
sesame seeds before they bake the cookies.

Glossary

communities Groups of people living in the same area

compassion Sorrow or pity for others

cycles Rotations of the Moon around Earth

dome A large rounded roof

fast To not eat

guidance The act or process of showing or explaining something to another

Islam A religion and a civilization

pilgrimage A journey

prophet A spiritual leader

purify To make clean

reinforce To build up or support something

revelation An act of making something known

tolerant The ability to accept feelings, habits, or beliefs that are different from one's own

translated Changed from one language into another

Index

32

Printed in the U.S.A.